SAVING YOUR SECOND MARRIAGE BEFORE IT STARTS

WORKBOOK FOR WOMEN

RESOURCES BY LES AND LESLIE PARROTT

3 Seconds (by Les)

The Complete Guide to Marriage Mentoring (and workbooks and video)

The Control Freak (by Les)

Crazy Good Sex (by Les)

Dot.com Dating

The First Drop of Rain (by Leslie)

Getting Ready for the Wedding

God Loves You Nose to Toes (children's book by Leslie)

The Good Fight

Helping Your Struggling Teenager (by Les)

High Maintenance Relationships (by Les)

The Hour That Matters Most

I Love You More (and workbooks and video)

L.O.V.E.

The Love List

Love Talk (and workbooks and video)

Love Talk Devotional

Making Happy

Meditations on Proverbs for Couples

The Parent You Want to Be

Questions Couples Ask

Real Relationships (and workbook and video)

Saving Your Marriage Before It Starts (and workbooks and video)

Saving Your Second Marriage Before It Starts (and workbooks and video)

Seven Secrets of a Healthy Dating Relationship (by Les)

Soul Friends (by Leslie)

Trading Places (and workbooks)

You Matter More Than You Think (by Leslie)

You're Stronger Than You Think (by Les)

Your Time-Starved Marriage (and workbooks and video)

SAVING YOUR SECOND MARRIAGE BEFORE IT STARTS

WORKBOOK FOR WOMEN

*Nine Questions to Ask Before —
and After — You Remarry*

NEWLY UPDATED EDITION

Drs. Les & Leslie Parrott
#1 *New York Times* Bestselling Authors

ZONDERVAN

Saving Your Second Marriage Before It Starts Workbook for Women
Copyright © 2001, 2006, 2015 by Les and Leslie Parrott

This title is also available as a Zondervan ebook. Visit www.zondervan.com/ebooks.

Requests for information should be addressed to:
Zondervan, 3900 *Sparks Dr. SE, Grand Rapids, Michigan* 49546

ISBN 978-0-310-87571-0

Published in association with Yates & Yates, www.yates2.com.

Cover design: Ranjy Thomas / Flying Rhino
Cover photography: Surkov Vladimir / Shutterstock®
Interior design: Kait Lamphere

First printing September 2015 / Printed in the United States of America

CONTENTS

SESSIONS

*For Group or Couple Discussion with
the Group Video Series*

HOW TO USE THIS WORKBOOK

WE HAVE SEEN MANY COUPLES who marry and then wait to see what will happen. This workbook is a tool to help you make the *right* things happen. Its brief exercises and activities, to be completed as you read through *Saving Your Second Marriage Before It Starts*, come from our work in counseling couples and are proven strategies for enriching and developing your relationship. Too often, reading a book can lead to great ideas, but little action. This workbook will help you put feet on the ideas and put them into action. And we believe you will enjoy it! As Shakespeare said, "Joy's soul lies in the doing."

TAKE THE SYMBIS ASSESSMENT

If you haven't done so already, we want to encourage you to take the SYMBIS Assessment. It's a perfect accompaniment to your workbook exercises. It takes just thirty minutes to complete online (each of you answers questions separately) and provides a powerful and personalized fifteen-page report. You'll discover your unique strengths as a couple and how your two personalities mesh. In short, the SYMBIS Assessment gives you every possible advantage for launching lifelong love, and it's sure to take your relationship to a deeper level of intimacy.

In fact, if you purchased the book, *Saving Your Second Marriage Before It Starts*, you can use the unique code (specific to the book) to obtain a discount.

Because the SYMBIS Assessment is so robust, you'll need a certified SYMBIS Facilitator to guide you through your results.[*]

Using the assessment is not required. It's simply an option. But we believe it is truly one of the best ways to make the content of the book and the exercises in this workbook deeply relevant to your relationship. If you are interested, simply go to SYMBISassessment.com to learn more.

You will also find several places in this workbook where we will point you to a particular section of your SYMBIS Assessment Report if you happen to be using it.

WHY IT'S IDEAL FOR EACH OF YOU TO HAVE YOUR OWN WORKBOOK

This workbook is to be used in conjunction with your partner—whether you're dating, engaged or newly married. There is one workbook designed for men and one for women, and it is important that each of you have your own copy. For the best results, each of you should work on the exercises separately, then meet together to discuss your answers. We know from working with countless couples that many of these exercises can serve as a potential epiphany for you—a real eye-opener—if you answer honestly (not trying to guess what your partner *wants* you to say).

This is why you'll get the most from these experiences if you each have your own copy of the workbook. In many places your answers would be influenced by seeing what your partner wrote and thus diminish the value of the exercise. In addition, the men's and women's workbooks are contextualized to each gender, and this one even has specific content for you as a woman.

---

[*] If you are already working with a counselor or pastor and they are not certified, we can help them become certified to use the assessment with you. They can do so at SYMBISassessment.com.

THE BEST APPROACH TO THESE EXERCISES

While there is no one right way to use this workbook, we suggest that you complete the exercises as you encounter them in the book, or soon after you have finished reading the chapter that covers the exercise. In other words, try to complete the exercises for that chapter before moving on to the next one. The point is to integrate the exercises into the process of reading the book. Some of the exercises are designed to be used again and again, helping you continue to improve your communication, for example, or deepen your sense of intimacy. Others are more of a one-shot exercise and are exploratory in nature.

In some cases, if you're using the SYMBIS Assessment, you may be using the workbooks with a SYMBIS Facilitator who will assign particular exercises as activities in between your sessions. And if you are debriefing your SYMBIS Assessment in a small group or class, you may use some of these exercises within the sessions themselves.

A NOTE ABOUT WORDING

We've designed these exercises to be appropriate for you—whether you are seriously dating, engaged, or already married. So don't get hung up on the use of "husband/wife" if you aren't married yet. We've done our best to avoid awkward phrasing while still acknowledging your relationship status. For example, we may say "partner" instead of "fiancé" or "spouse," etc.

USING THESE WORKBOOKS LONG-DISTANCE

If you and your partner are not in close proximity at this time, you can still do these exercises together. In fact, we have heard from countless couples who are in the military or located in different cities for various reasons during their engagement period or early years of marriage, and they love doing these exercises long-distance. They create a meaningful point of connection even when miles separate you.

As you navigate through the pages of this workbook, make it your own. Don't get too hung up on following the rules. If a particular exercise leads you down a more intriguing path, take it. Some of these exercises may simply serve as a springboard to discussions that fit your style more appropriately. However, if an exercise seems a bit challenging, don't give up on it. As the saying goes, anything worth having is worth working for. In any case, the goal of this workbook is not simply to fortify your reading of *Saving Your Second Marriage Before It Starts*—the goal is to apply it to your relationship, to make it stick.

A QUICK NOTE
TO LEADERS

WE KNOW THAT MANY LEADERS use these his/her workbooks to augment their sessions with couples. That's fantastic. With that in mind, we want to be sure you are aware of two resources that can be particularly helpful to you and the couples you serve.

If you are a certified SYMBIS Facilitator, you already know that the exercises in this workbook fit hand in glove with the personalized content found in the SYMBIS Assessment. If you are a minister, counselor or marriage mentor couple and you are not yet certified as a SYMBIS Facilitator, you can become one in no time. Simply visit SYMBISassessment.com for more information on how you can begin your training.

If you are leading a group or class of couples, the DVD kit that accompanies *Saving Your Second Marriage Before It Starts* can be especially helpful. For this reason, we have included a "Discussion Guide" in the later portion of these workbooks. The materials in your DVD kit as well as the resources in your online dashboard as a SYMBIS Facilitator will provide you with more guidance on optimizing your group experiences.

EXERCISES

---

*28 Self-Tests to Put
the Book into Action*

Exercise One

THE REMARRIAGE MOTIVATION TEST

ON A SCALE OF 1 TO 10, rate how much of a factor each of the following motivators are for you to get married. Take time to consider each item, and be as honest as possible.

1. Love at first sight is a factor in why I'm ready to get married again.

Not at All True   Extremely True of Me

1	2	3	4	5	6	7	8	9	10

2. Rebounding from the pain of a previous marriage is a factor in my motivation for this second marriage.

Not at All True   Extremely True of Me

1	2	3	4	5	6	7	8	9	10

3. Rebellion against my ex-husband is a factor in my motivation.

Not at All True   Extremely True of Me

1	2	3	4	5	6	7	8	9	10

4. Loneliness contributes to my reasons for getting married again.

Not at All True   Extremely True of Me

1	2	3	4	5	6	7	8	9	10

5. A sense of obligation is a factor in motivating me to marry.

Not at All True   Extremely True of Me

1	2	3	4	5	6	7	8	9	10

6. Financial advancement is a part of my decision to get remarried.

Not at All True   Extremely True of Me

1	2	3	4	5	6	7	8	9	10

7. Sexual attraction is a factor driving me to get married at this time.

Not at All True   Extremely True of Me

1	2	3	4	5	6	7	8	9	10

8. Escape from an unhappy first marriage is causing me to want to get married again.

Not at All True   Extremely True of Me

1	2	3	4	5	6	7	8	9	10

9. Pressure from others has something to do with why I am getting married again.

Not at All True   Extremely True of Me

1	2	3	4	5	6	7	8	9	10

Scoring: Add up your score from each of the nine items. There are 90 possible points on this test. Add 10 to your score. If your score is 50 or less, you can rest easy in the fact that you are probably not getting remarried for some of the most common negative reasons. If your score is greater than 50, you will certainly want to do some soul-searching on your own and with your partner about the items that you ranked highest. We also strongly suggest talking about these motivators with an objective counselor.

Exercise Two

THE REMARRIAGE READINESS QUESTIONNAIRE

IF YOU HAVE TAKEN the SYMBIS Assessment (SYMBISassessment.com), this particular exercise will look familiar. The SYMBIS Assessment Report presents the content of this exercise in a far more personalized format. If you're not using the SYMBIS Assessment, however, you will still benefit significantly from this workbook version of the exercise.

The following questions will help you assess your readiness for remarriage. Be ruthlessly honest with yourself while answering these questions.

1. Do you know who you are and do you like who you are?

2. Would you say you generally have a healthy sense of self-esteem and confidence?

3. Do you feel comfortable talking about your differences in times of conflict (rather than ignoring them)?

4. Are you twenty years of age or older?

5. Are you twenty-four years of age or older?

6. Would people you respect say you are personally mature?

7. Would you say you have resolved most of the ugly issues with your former husband?

8. Do you feel comfortable thinking for yourself and making your own decisions?

9. Are you able to make decisions without feeling compelled to please others?

10. Are you genuinely prepared to make your marriage relationship of utmost priority?

11. Have you resolved painful or other troubling issues with your past that are bound to impact your new marriage?

12. Have you identified specific quirks or qualities you may be bringing into your marriage as a result of your previous relationship?

13. Have you dated your partner for a year or more?

14. Have you dated your partner for two years or more?

15. Are you willing to take your time in determining whether your relationship is really ready for marriage?

16. Would you characterize your relationship as stable and steadfast?

17. Do you both practice compromise and negotiation effectively in your relationship?

18. Can you both resolve conflict between you without losing control?

19. Are you 100 percent committed, beyond a shadow of a doubt, to making this relationship work?

20. Do you fully agree with your partner's important goals and values?

21. Do you and your partner share many similarities (e.g., sense of humor, habits, goals)?

22. Are your differences tiny compared to your similarities?

23. Do you and your partner have similar family backgrounds?

24. Do you and your partner refrain from criticizing, correcting, or trying to "fix" each other?

25. Do you like this person as he is at this moment (as compared to expecting him to change)?

Scoring: Add up the number of yes responses from these items and multiply by four. That will give you a possible score of 100. If you answered honestly and your score is 90 or higher, your answers indicate you are probably ready for remarriage. A score of 80 to 89 indicates that you are on your way but would probably be wise to give it more time and careful counsel. A score of 79 or lower indicates that you still have a great deal of work to do before you are ready for remarriage. You are likely to benefit from the help of a good counselor and more time. Whether your score is high or low, this brief self-report assessment should serve simply as a guideline, not as the final answer.

Exercise Three

YOUR PERSONAL TEN COMMANDMENTS

THIS EXERCISE IS DESIGNED to help you uncover some of your unspoken rules. It will take about fifteen to twenty minutes.

Try to articulate some of the unspoken rules you grew up with. Take your time to think it over. These unspoken rules are generally so ingrained that we are rarely aware of them. If you're not married yet, by the way, you may have discovered some of your "rules" with a previous roommate.

We've provided you with sections to stimulate your thinking. The best way to come up with your own commandments is to think of what "unspoken rules" you grew up with in your family.

RULES ABOUT FINANCES

Example: "Credit cards are to be used only in an emergency."

1. _____

_____

2. _____

_____

RULES ABOUT MEALTIME

Example: "Dinner should be served at the same time every night."

3. _____

_____

4. _____

_____

RULES ABOUT CHORES

Example: "The towels from the laundry should be folded in thirds (not in half)."

5. _____

_____

6. _____

_____

RULES ABOUT OTHER TRADITIONS AND HOLIDAYS

Example: "You should open presents on Christmas Eve (not Christmas morning)."

7. _____

_____

8. _____

_____

RULES ABOUT QUIRKY THINGS

Example: "Never put a bottle of ketchup on the table (put it in a dish)."

9. _____

_____

10. _____

_____

Once both of you have written your "personal ten commandments," share them with each other.

As a woman, think about how your mom modeled certain behaviors in each of these areas and consider how this may shape your expectations as a wife.

What surprises you about your partner's rules and why? Do some of his rules cause you to immediately push back?

Are there any specific rules you would like to change (on your side or his)?

The more you talk about your unspoken rules, the less likely they are to affect your marriage in a negative way.

In addition, here's a helpful tip. Any time you have a fight or disagreement, ask yourself, "Is this fight a result of one of us breaking an unspoken rule?" If so, add that rule to your list and discuss how you will handle that situation in the future.

Exercise Four

MAKING YOUR ROLES CONSCIOUS

IF YOU ARE USING the SYMBIS Assessment, a portion of a page of your fifteen-page report personalizes the results of this particular workbook exercise, so you may want to refer to that page now. Either way, this exercise will help you evaluate role expectations in your own terms and then compare your expectations with your partner's.

Following is a list of chores or life tasks that will need to be handled by you or your fiancé (husband). To make your unconscious understanding of roles conscious, first indicate how your parents handled these tasks. If they shared the task, then check both boxes. Then write down how you would like to divide the tasks, according to your understanding of your own and your partner's interests, time, and abilities. If you expect to share the task, check both boxes. Finally, compare your list with your partner's list and discuss the results. Put your joint decision of who will do what in the last column, and be prepared to renegotiate when your circumstances change. This exercise will take about twenty to thirty minutes.

	Your Mother	Your Father	You	Your Spouse	Final Decision
Providing income	☐	☐	☐	☐	_____
Staying home with children	☐	☐	☐	☐	_____
Paying bills and handling finances	☐	☐	☐	☐	_____
Yard work	☐	☐	☐	☐	_____
Gassing up the car	☐	☐	☐	☐	_____
Automobile maintenance	☐	☐	☐	☐	_____
Fixing things around the house	☐	☐	☐	☐	_____
Laundry	☐	☐	☐	☐	_____
Making the bed	☐	☐	☐	☐	_____
Doing the dishes	☐	☐	☐	☐	_____
Cleaning	☐	☐	☐	☐	_____
Cooking and baking	☐	☐	☐	☐	_____
Taking out the trash	☐	☐	☐	☐	_____
Grocery shopping	☐	☐	☐	☐	_____
Caring for a pet	☐	☐	☐	☐	_____
Scheduling social events	☐	☐	☐	☐	_____
Maintaining ties with friends and relatives	☐	☐	☐	☐	_____
Planning vacations	☐	☐	☐	☐	_____
Talking about spiritual matters	☐	☐	☐	☐	_____
Decorating the house	☐	☐	☐	☐	_____
Making major decisions	☐	☐	☐	☐	_____

	Your Mother	Your Father	You	Your Spouse	Final Decision
Initiating discussion about the relationship	☐	☐	☐	☐	_____
Keeping the house neat and orderly	☐	☐	☐	☐	_____
Disciplining the children	☐	☐	☐	☐	_____
Shopping for other needs	☐	☐	☐	☐	_____
Other _____	☐	☐	☐	☐	_____
Other _____	☐	☐	☐	☐	_____

Once you have both filled out this list, compare notes and answer these three questions together:

1. What role behaviors do you tend to agree upon?

2. What role behaviors do you tend to see quite differently?

3. How are you going to adjust your expectations on the role behaviors where you are currently not in sync?

Exercise Five

FROM IDEALIZING TO REALIZING YOUR PARTNER

THIS EXERCISE IS DESIGNED to help you relinquish unrealistic ideals you might hold about your partner and to discover his true character. It will take about twenty to thirty minutes.

Begin by rating on a 1 to 7 scale (1 being lowest and 7 being highest) how much the following traits describe you and your partner. Complete the first two columns ("Your Rating of You" and then "Your Rating of Your Husband"). Don't worry about the other two columns just yet.

Your Rating of You		Your Rating of Your Husband		Your Husband's Actual Rating		The Difference
___	Compassionate	___	-	___	=	___
___	Patient	___	-	___	=	___
___	Secure	___	-	___	=	___
___	Nurturing	___	-	___	=	___
___	Insightful	___	-	___	=	___
___	Confident	___	-	___	=	___
___	Relaxed	___	-	___	=	___
___	Tender	___	-	___	=	___
___	Even tempered	___	-	___	=	___

Your Rating of You		Your Rating of Your Husband		Your Husband's Actual Rating		The Difference
___	Honest	___	-	___	=	___
___	Healthy	___	-	___	=	___
___	Spiritual	___	-	___	=	___
___	Consistent	___	-	___	=	___

Once you have rated the first two columns, share your rating with each other and write them on your own page. Then subtract your partner's actual rating of himself from your rating of her. Note any significant differences and discuss them.

Our three biggest differences in this exercise are:

1. _____

_____

2. _____

_____

3. _____

_____

One of the central tasks of the early marriage years is to move from "idealizing" your husband to "realizing" your husband. How accurate is your image of who your husband is compared to who he really is? The more accurately you can present yourselves to each other, the easier your first years of marriage will be.

Exercise Six

EXPLORING UNFINISHED BUSINESS

MARRIAGE IS NOT A QUICK FIX for avoiding your own personal problems. In fact, marriage may even intensify those problems. This exercise is designed to help you honestly face the psychological and spiritual work you need to do as a person so that you do not look to your husband to fulfill needs that he cannot. It will take about twenty to thirty minutes.

Everyone has yearnings that were seldom, if ever, fulfilled in their relationship with their parents. Take a moment to reflect, and then write down some of the needs and desires you felt that were never really fulfilled by your parents. We've provided you with a few headings to stimulate your thinking, but don't let that limit you to just these categories.

UNFULFILLED NEEDS FOR ENCOURAGEMENT

Example: "My parents never really encouraged my dreams or goals."

....

....

....

UNFULFILLED NEEDS FOR PRAISE

Example: "My parents never really celebrated my successes."

_____

_____

_____

UNFULFILLED NEEDS FOR LISTENING

Example: "My parents never really understood me for who I am."

_____

_____

_____

UNFULFILLED NEEDS FOR FUN

Example: "My parents often thought I wasn't serious enough and wanted me to be more 'goal oriented.'"

_____

_____

_____

OTHER UNFULFILLED NEEDS THAT SHAPE MY EXPECTATIONS

Example: "I've never had anyone in my life who appreciates my creativity."

_____

_____

_____

When we marry, we long to recreate the love and closeness and nurturance that we experienced or wished we had experienced in our relationship with our parents. But marriage is not always the place for those yearnings to be fulfilled. No human can meet another person's every need; deep relational longings are ultimately met only in a relationship with God.

If you are willing, share your writing with your partner and discuss the baggage you are both bringing into your marriage—and how your expectations of him as your husband might be shaped by your "unfinished business."

Exercise Seven

ASSESSING YOUR SELF-IMAGE

THIS EXERCISE IS DESIGNED to help you measure your self-image and construct an interdependent relationship with your husband. It will take about twenty to thirty minutes.

"You cannot love another person unless you love yourself." Most of us have heard that statement so often we tend to dismiss it as just another catchphrase in the lexicon of pop psychology. But a solid sense of self-esteem is a vital element in building the capacity to love.

The following self-test can give you a quick evaluation of your self-esteem. Answer each with "yes," "usually," "seldom," or "no."

1. Do you believe strongly in certain values and principles, enough that you are willing to defend them?

Yes	Usually	Seldom	No

2. Do you act on your own best judgment, without regretting your actions if others disapprove?

Yes	Usually	Seldom	No

3. Do you avoid worrying about what is coming tomorrow or fussing over yesterday's or today's mistakes?

Yes	Usually	Seldom	No

4. Do you have confidence in your general ability to deal with problems, even in the face of failures and setbacks?

Yes	Usually	Seldom	No

5. Do you feel generally equal — neither inferior nor superior — to others?

Yes	Usually	Seldom	No

6. Do you take it more or less for granted that other people are interested in you and value you?

Yes	Usually	Seldom	No

7. Do you accept praise without pretense or false modesty, and accept compliments without feeling guilty?

Yes	Usually	Seldom	No

8. Do you resist the efforts of others to dominate you, especially your peers?

Yes	Usually	Seldom	No

9. Do you accept the idea — and admit to others — that you are capable of feeling a wide range of impulses and desires, ranging from anger to love, sadness to happiness, resentment to acceptance? (It does not follow, however, that you will act on all these feelings and desires.)

Yes	Usually	Seldom	No

10. Do you genuinely enjoy yourself in a wide range of activities, including work, play, creative self-expression, companionship, and just plain loafing?

Yes	Usually	Seldom	No

11. Do you sense and consider the needs of others?

Yes	Usually	Seldom	No

If your answer to most of the questions is "yes" or "usually," it's an indication that you have a sturdy sense of self-esteem. If most of your answers are "no" or "seldom," you may likely suffer from a low self-image and will need to strengthen it to build the best marriage. Research indicates that self-esteem has a lot to do with the way you will respond to your wife. People with a healthy self-image are more apt to express their opinions, are less sensitive to criticism, and are generally less preoccupied with themselves.

The point of this little self-test is not to accurately pinpoint your self-esteem. It's to generate a helpful discussion between the two of you. So, if you are willing, discuss your answers with each other and talk about how in reality you cannot make each other whole (though you can certainly help each other on the pathway to wholeness).

Exercise Eight

DEFINING LOVE

IF YOU ARE USING the SYMBIS Assessment, a portion of a page of your fifteen-page SYMBIS Report personalizes the results of this particular workbook exercise, so you may want to refer to that page now. Either way, this exercise will help you define love in your own terms and compare your definition with your partner's. It will take ten to fifteen minutes.

Researcher Beverly Fehr asked more than 170 people to rate the central features of love.

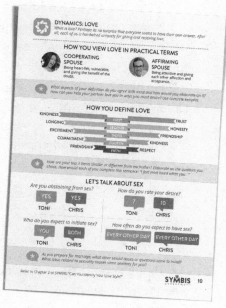

The twelve most important attributes they identified are listed below. Take a moment to prioritize this list for yourself by check-marking the three qualities that are most important to you.

___ Acceptance

___ Caring

___ Commitment

___ Concern for the other's well-being

___ Friendship

___ Honesty

___ Interest in the other

___ Loyalty

___ Respect

___ Supportiveness

___ Trust

___ Wanting to be with the other

Next, write a brief definition of love that incorporates these qualities.

Love is . . .

_____

_____

_____

Now, compare your priorities and your definition with your partner's to see what differences, if any, you might have when it comes to defining love.

Finally, complete these sentences to get a better feel for the application of your definition of love:

I feel most loved when you . . .

_____

_____

_____

Though you may or may not know it, I'm showing you my love when I . . .

_____

_____

_____

If pertinent to you: My definition of love has changed in the following ways since my first marriage . . .

_____

_____

_____

GETTING YOUR SEX LIFE OFF TO A GREAT START

THIS EXERCISE IS DESIGNED to help you dispel some common myths about sex and become more knowledgeable about lovemaking as a married couple.*

Below is a true and false questionnaire for you to complete. Don't worry about getting the right answers. Simply answer each item the best you can.

T   F   The key to sexual fulfillment is simply to do what comes naturally. In other words, let your instincts be your guide.

T   F   Most normal married couples have sexual intercourse about two to three times a week.

T   F   Because men typically have a stronger sex drive than women, it is primarily the husband's job to initiate sex — not the wife's.

T   F   When it comes down to it, men are almost always ready and willing to have sex, and a good wife should always be available for it.

T   F   The best way for a woman to have an orgasm is during intercourse.

---

* We are indebted to Cliff and Joyce Penner and Louis and Melissa McBurney for the wealth of knowledge they provide in this area.

T   F   While men have just one orgasm during sex, a woman must have multiple orgasms to be fulfilled sexually.

T   F   A man's erection is a signal that he is going to need intercourse or ejaculation.

T   F   The normal position for sexual intercourse is with the man on top.

T   F   To reach ultimate sexual fulfillment, a couple should strive for simultaneous orgasms, where both the husband and wife climax at the same time.

T   F   In general, the larger the man's penis, the more pleasurable sex is for the woman.

Number of True answers: ____   Number of False answers: ____

Once you have totaled your answers, compare notes and go through the following correct answers together. What matters here is not whether you answered correctly—the point is to learn more accurate information about your sex life as a married couple.

T   F   The key to sexual fulfillment is simply to do what comes naturally. In other words, let your instincts be your guide.

While many believe that if you are really good at sex you don't have to learn about it, the truth is that good sex requires much more than just doing what comes naturally. Therefore, one of the best ways to improve your sex life after marriage and to really enjoy it is to educate yourselves, experiment with each other, and teach each other. For example, this may mean reading a book from time to time about sexual intimacy in marriage. The more you learn about sex as a couple, especially each other's preferences and desires, the better your sex life will be. So the answer to this item is false.

| T | F | Most normal married couples have sexual intercourse about two to three times a week. |

When it comes to the frequency of sexual intercourse in your marriage, the two of you determine what is normal. You may have sex twice a day or twice per month. What matters is that, over the course of your married life, you talk about the best balance of your two sexual desires. So the answer to this item is false.

| T | F | Because men typically have a stronger sex drive than women, it is primarily the husband's job to initiate sex — not the wife's. |

Women have sexual urges and thoughts just as men do. In fact, women tend to fantasize even more than men. When women learn to express their sexual urges directly and share their creative fantasies, their husbands are delighted and their sex life is sparked. So it's not up to the man to always initiate sex, and the answer to this item is false. By the way, since women can be more particular about where, when, and how they want to be touched, it takes pressure off the husband and produces greater pleasure for the wife if she also takes the lead.

| T | F | When it comes down to it, men are almost always ready and willing to have sex, and a good wife should always be available for it. |

Yikes! This false belief has led too many couples into trouble because it produces such incredible demand — on both partners. First, it demands that the husband behave as though he is interested even when he is not. And it also demands that the wife be responsive to her husband's arousal even when she is not interested. Truth be told, either one of you can decide to participate in a sexual time together when one of you is feeling the desire and the other is not, but it should not be by demand. Sex should always be a choice. As the Penners say, "Demand is a killer to a healthy, long-term sexual relationship."

T   F   The best way for a woman to have an orgasm is during intercourse.

Here's the truth: The majority of women do not have orgasms during intercourse. While any woman can learn to be orgasmic during intercourse if she desires to, most women respond orgasmically to manual clitoral stimulation. Of course, some women only respond during intercourse and others respond either way. All variations are delightful ways of receiving sexual pleasure and release, but have nothing to do with "the right way." What is right is what works for you. And keep in mind that the stimulation that triggers the orgasm in the woman has nothing to do with the man or his masculinity. As you both listen to your inner desires and communicate those desires to each other and respond to each other's invitations, the automatic response orgasm is more likely to happen. So the answer to this item is false.

T   F   While men have just one orgasm during sex, a woman must have multiple orgasms to be fulfilled sexually.

The number of orgasms a woman experiences during sex is not an indicator of her level of sexual fulfillment. Many women are totally satisfied after one release. Others quickly get restimulated and desire more. So, for the man, there's no need to equate the number of orgasms with his level of "performance." So the answer to this item is false.

T F A man's erection is a signal that he is going to need inter-course or ejaculation.

An erection simply means a man is aroused and that's all. An erection for the man is no different than vaginal lubrication for the woman. It's not a demand for action, even though many men say they just cannot handle getting aroused and not having an ejaculation. The truth is that all men get erections every eighty to ninety minutes while they sleep, but these erections rarely lead to an ejaculation. It is equally possible to allow arousal to come and go during caressing or in response to seeing his wife's body. So, again, the answer to this item is false.

T F The normal position for sexual intercourse is with the man on top.

The man-on-top position is commonly used by many couples, but that does not make it the normal or right position. With more sexual experiences together in your marriage, you will discover positions that bring you the most pleasure. You need to feel free to try a variety of positions in your lovemaking. So the answer is false.

T F To reach ultimate sexual fulfillment, a couple should strive for simultaneous orgasms, where both the husband and wife climax at the same time.

Having simultaneous orgasms can be fun if it happens, but it's an unnecessary goal to put on your lovemaking. It has absolutely nothing to do with how successful you are as a couple. The demand for both spouses to have orgasms at the same time gets in the way of the pleasure of enjoying each other. Many couples prefer separate orgasms so each one can experience the other's. So, again, the answer is false.

Penis size is the source of many myths. But in truth, it has nothing to do with a man's sexuality, his attractiveness to his wife, his skill
as a lover, or the satisfaction he can bring to his wife. The quality of
sex is not in any way related to penis size. When erect, penises vary
little in size from one to another. A smaller, flaccid penis enlarges
proportionately more when erect than does a larger flaccid penis.
Also, the vagina adapts to the penis, and it is only in the outer third
of the vagina that the woman responds to the penis. The shortest
penis is more than adequate to bring pleasure to a woman. So the
answer is false. The penis myths perpetuated by locker-room jokes
have nothing to do with reality.

So, each of the ten items in this self-test is false. If you answered
any of them as true, don't feel badly. Each of these items represents
one of the most common myths about marital sex. And now that you
know the truth, you are far more likely to get your sex life off to a
great start.

Of course, to augment your sexual knowledge, you will also need
a solid understanding of the male and female anatomy. You have
probably already studied this in school, but even so, it's very helpful
to brush up on this information. Cliff and Joyce Penner's bestselling
book *The Gift of Sex* is a terrific resource for this, as is Louis and
Melissa McBurney's book *Real Questions, Real Answers about Sex*.

We want to leave you with one more thought. Remember that
one of the keys to a great sex life is to talk openly about it as husband
and wife. Far too many married couples simply don't discuss their sex
life together. Once you are married, we recommend that you talk in
specific terms by completing such sentences as:

I feel sexually aroused by you when . . .
When we are making love, I really enjoy . . .
When we are making love, I feel uncomfortable when you . . .

The surest turnoff for me is . . .
The surest turn-on for me is . . .
What you need to know about me when it comes to sex is . . .

These kinds of specific statements will do wonders for your sex life right from the start and ensure "hot monogamy" for decades.

Exercise Ten

YOUR CHANGING LOVE STYLE

THIS EXERCISE WILL HELP YOU understand how love is not stagnant and how the love you have for each other will change during different life passages. It will take twenty-five to thirty minutes.

Using the triangular model of love described in chapter 3 of *Saving Your Second Marriage Before It Starts* (passion, intimacy, and commitment), draw how your love style with your partner has changed over time. You may want to divide your relationship into three phases and then draw the love triangle that best suits each phase. In other words, if early on passion was stronger than commitment and intimacy, draw a triangle (identifying each side) representing that, and so on.

First third of our relationship

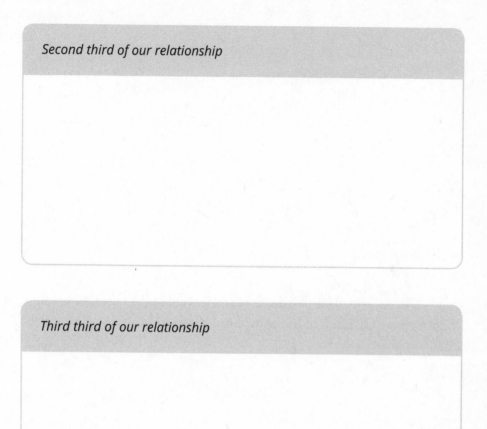

Second third of our relationship

Third third of our relationship

As we grow and develop, each stage of the life cycle is marked by the emergence of a new form of love. This means that during certain phases of life, some sides of the triangle will get more attention than others. Using the triangular model of love, on the next page draw how your love might look in future passages of marriage (e.g., how will it look in five years or even fifty years).

Discuss with your partner how you feel about the inevitability of love taking on different forms in your future.

Exercise Eleven

CULTIVATING INTIMACY

THIS EXERCISE WILL HELP YOU open your heart and increase your level of intimacy.

Begin by writing about your shared experiences. What is it about your backgrounds that draws you together? What things set the two of you apart from others? What experiences have you had together that bring back fond memories?

Next, focus on things that the two of you share. Begin by jotting down one or two things in each of the following categories, then discuss them with your partner. The more detailed you can be, the better.

- Interests we have in common include:

_____

_____

_____

- Plans we share for our future include:

_____

_____

_____

- Fears and anxieties we both have include:

_____

_____

_____

- Hopes and dreams we share include:

_____

_____

_____

- Spiritual beliefs we both have include:

_____

_____

_____

Conclude this exercise by talking in specific terms about what the two of you can do to cultivate more emotional intimacy in your relationship.

LISTENING TO YOUR SELF-TALK

THIS EXERCISE WILL HELP YOU and your partner examine how much your attitude shapes the moods of your marriage. It will take about ten to fifteen minutes.

List three circumstances that typically get you into a rotten mood. For example: being stuck in traffic, waiting for someone who is late to arrive, having your credit card rejected, and so on.

1. _____

_____

2. _____

_____

3. _____

_____

There is a maxim in psychology that says "you feel what you think." In other words, your feelings are the result of what is going on in your mind. For each of the bad circumstances you listed above, write down what you are saying to yourself that makes you feel so rotten. For example: "I could be playing tennis instead of being stuck on this freeway."

1. _____

_____

2. _____

_____

3. _____

_____

Now, exercise your power to choose your own attitude by changing your self-talk. Write three alternative statements that would not lead to feeling so rotten. For example: "At least I can use this time to just relax and mentally rehearse my tennis serve."

1. _____

_____

2. _____

_____

3. _____

_____

Negative self-talk can also affect our responses to more serious situations. To see how negative self-talk may have affected you, list two situations in your life that were difficult or painful to deal with. For example: losing a job, breaking off a relationship, or going through a serious illness.

1. _____

_____

2. _____

_____

For each of the crises you listed above, write down things you said to yourself that added to your pain. For example: "I was fired from my job because I'm a natural-born loser."

1. _____

_____

2. _____

_____

Again, exercise your power to choose your own attitude by changing your self-talk. Write two alternative statements that did help or could have helped you adapt to the situation and grow through it. For example: "I will learn from my mistakes and, with God's help, make sure they don't happen again."

1. _____

_____

2. _____

_____

Talk about this exercise with your partner. Discuss how changing your self-talk can improve your chances for marital happiness. How can the two of you team up to fight negative self-talk?

AVOIDING THE BLAME GAME

THIS EXERCISE WILL HELP YOU and your partner take responsibility for your own attitudes. It will take about ten to fifteen minutes.

Below are several scenarios where blame typically enters the picture. For each scenario, decide on your own who is to blame.

FIRST SCENE

It's Valentine's Day. Mary has prepared a special meal for Dan—all his favorite foods. She also made him a special valentine. Dan, however, didn't get Mary anything. After dinner, Dan thanks Mary for the food and slumps into a chair in front of the television. Mary, feeling hurt, leaves the dirty dishes in the sink and goes into the bedroom to cry. Dan realizes what just happened, follows her into the bedroom, and the two accuse each other of being insensitive. Who is at fault?

Dan is to blame   Mary is to blame

SECOND SCENE

Aaron and Kim are having dinner with another couple. During the casual conversation, Kim jokingly makes fun of Aaron's shirt. He laughs at first but soon he becomes withdrawn, and the conversation becomes noticeably strained. When they get home, both of them accuse the other of ruining the evening. Who is at fault?

Aaron is to blame   Kim is to blame

THIRD SCENE

On a whim, Carl buys a new hi-def TV on sale. He and Michelle had talked about getting one, but they'd decided to wait another year. Carl, however, felt the bargain was too good to pass up and also thought it would be a nice surprise for Michelle. It wasn't. All Michelle could think about was how they were saving money for plane tickets to see her family at Christmas. Carl and Michelle blamed each other for being too controlling with their money. Who is at fault?

Carl is to blame   Michelle is to blame

You may now compare your answers with each other, but there are no "correct" responses. It doesn't matter who is to blame. It doesn't matter who is at fault. What matters in building a happy marriage is defining what the problem is and seeing how each of you can be a part of the solution. Take time to read through the scenarios again, placing yourselves in each couple's shoes. What could each of you do to avoid playing the blame game in these instances?

_____

_____

_____

_____

_____

_____

_____

Exercise Fourteen

ADJUSTING TO THINGS BEYOND YOUR CONTROL

IF YOU ARE USING the SYMBIS Assessment you may want to refer to the Dynamics: Attitude page of your personalized report as it relates to this particular workbook exercise. This one will help you and your partner more effectively adjust to the jolts of life. It will take about ten to fifteen minutes.

The book talked about how different the Christmas story would be if Mary and Joseph had not had the capacity to adjust to circumstances beyond their con-

trol. What situations or circumstances in your relationship (including your wedding if you are already married) have already thrown you for a loop? Jot down two or three particular challenges you did not anticipate:

_____

_____

_____

55

How did you respond to these unexpected situations? List some things you did to keep your chin up and some things you did that didn't work as well.

Positive Ways I Coped	Negative Ways I Coped

Now compare your coping strategies with your partner's. In what ways can the two of you improve your capacities to adjust? How can you be better equipped to maintain a positive outlook when similar unexpected circumstances arise in the future?

Conclude this exercise by discussing what will happen in your marriage if you do not practice your ability to adjust to things beyond your control.

Exercise Fifteen

HOW WELL DO YOU COMMUNICATE?

IF YOU ARE USING the SYMBIS Assessment you may want to refer to the Dynamics: Communication page of your report as it relates to your personal "talk styles." It will provide fuller context to this exercise which is designed to help you improve how well you communicate with your partner. It will take about ten minutes. Answer the questions as honestly as you can. The more honest you are, the more meaningful the exercise will be.

1. The anniversary of your first date is coming up. You have always remembered it and it is important to you, but your partner often forgets, so you:

   A. Wait to see if he'll remember.

   B. Drop hints.

   C. Remind him.

2. If you have a problem with your husband, with whom will you first discuss it?

   A. No one

   B. A friend or close relative

   C. Him

3. He really hurt your feelings. Do you:

   A. Tell him so?

   B. Give him the cold shoulder for a while?

   C. Lash out and hurt him back?

4. If something terribly embarrassing happened to you, would you tell your husband about it?

   A. No

   B. Maybe

   C. Probably

5. Baseball bores you to death, but your husband could discuss it for hours. When the subject comes up, you:

   A. Explain how bored you are and ask him to talk about something else.

   B. Change the subject as soon as possible.

   C. Work on showing some interest.

6. You had an unsuccessful job interview at lunchtime, and you're very upset. When you see your husband later than evening, he looks downcast. You:

   A. Wait until he's in a better mood to tell him about it.

   B. Tell him you didn't get the job but try to hide your emotional reaction.

   C. Begin pouring out your story the moment you see him.

7. For the second time this month your husband has broken a promise to take you to a play. Do you:

A. Break a promise you've made to see how he likes it?

B. Sulk and tell him how inconsiderate he is?

C. Adjust to the letdown but tell him you are annoyed?

Scoring: For questions one, two, four, five, and seven, give yourself one point for each "A" answer, two for each "B," and three for each "C." Then on questions three and six, give yourself three points for each "A," two for each "B," and one for each "C."

7 to 11 points: You need some help in learning how to communicate more effectively. You may have a tendency to become defensive and impatient. Chapter 6 will show you how to improve your skills.

12 to 17 points: You are not doing badly, but there are some sensitive spots in your makeup that tend to block communication. You could really benefit from practicing some of the skills discussed in chapter 6.

18 to 21 points: You're doing quite well in the area of communication, but there's always room for improvement. Chapter 6 will help you fine-tune some skills you are already good at.

Exercise Sixteen

THE DAILY TEMPERATURE READING

THIS EXERCISE WILL HELP YOU and your partner maintain an easy flow of communication about the big and little things going on in your lives. It will take about thirty minutes.

At first this exercise may seem artificial and even hokey. But in time you'll evolve your own style and find that it is invaluable for staying close. Do it daily, perhaps during a meal. Here are the basics. Sit close, holding each other's hands (touch creates an atmosphere of acceptance), then follow these five steps:

1. *Appreciation.* Take turns expressing appreciation for something your partner has done. Thank each other.

_____

_____

2. *New Information.* In the absence of information, assumptions (often false ones) rush in. Tell your partner something new ("We finally got a new account executive at work"). Let your partner in on your life, and then listen to the news your partner shares.

_____

_____

3. *Puzzles.* Take turns asking each other something you don't under-stand but your partner can explain: "Why were you so down last night?" Or voice a concern about yourself: "I don't know why I got so angry while I was balancing the checkbook yesterday."

_____

_____

4. *Complaint with Request.* Without being judgmental, cite a specific behavior that bothers you and state the behavior you are asking for instead. "When you clean the top of the stove, please dry it with a paper towel. If you don't, it leaves streaks."

_____

_____

5. *Hopes.* Share your hopes, from the mundane ("I hope we have sunshine this weekend") to the grandiose ("I'd really love to spend a month in Europe with you").

_____

_____

These simple steps have worked for many couples who want to keep the channels of communication open.

I CAN HEAR CLEARLY NOW

YOUR PARTNER WILL OFTEN hide important feelings behind his words. Reflecting his feelings is one of the most helpful and difficult listening techniques to implement. Following are some statements that a husband might make. Read each separately, listening for feelings. Make note of the feeling you hear, and write out a response which reflects that feeling for each of the statements.

1. "I can't believe you agreed to go on this deal tonight without asking me first."

_____

_____

2. "Can't I relax a minute before we head out again?"

_____

_____

3. "Why can't you get ready in the same time I do? It seems like I'm always waiting for you."

_____

_____

4. "Everyone at work seems to be moving up but me."

_____

_____

5. "What's the use? I can't seem to get through to him, so why try?"

_____

_____

Now compare your list of reflective statements to those listed below to see how accurately you recognized feelings. Give yourself a 2 on those items where your choice closely matches, a 1 on items where your choice only partially matches, and a 0 if you missed altogether.

Possible Responses to the Exercise in Active Listening:

1. "Sounds like you are feeling betrayed."
2. "Sounds like you need some time to calm down and recover."
3. "You sound frustrated. I appreciate your patience."
4. "You must feel like you're getting passed over."
5. "Sounds like you're giving up hope."

How You Rate on Recognizing Feelings:

8–10   Above average recognition of feelings
5–7   Average recognition of feelings
0–4   Below average recognition of feelings

Exercise Eighteen

COUPLE'S INVENTORY

_____

THIS EXERCISE WILL HELP YOU take stock of the roles you both play, consciously and unconsciously, in your relationship. It will take about twenty to thirty minutes.

Complete the following sentences as honestly as you can.

1. I am important to our marriage because _____

_____

_____

2. What I contribute to my partner's success is _____

_____

_____

3. I feel central to our relationship when _____

_____

_____

4. I feel peripheral to our relationship when _____

_____

_____

5. The ways I have fun with you are _____

_____

_____

6. The way I get space for myself in our relationship is _____

_____

_____

7. The ways I am intimate with you are _____

_____

_____

8. The role I play as your wife is _____

_____

_____

9. I feel most feminine in our relationship when _____

_____

_____

10. I deal with stress by _____

_____

_____

11. The division of labor in household tasks is decided by _____

_____

_____

12. Our finances are controlled by _____

_____

_____

13. How we spend our spare time is determined by _____

_____

_____

14. Our social life is planned by _____

_____

_____

15. I need you to _____

_____

_____

Compare your statements with each other and discuss how being a woman influences the way you responded.

Exercise Nineteen

YOUR TOP TEN NEEDS

IF YOU ARE USING the SYMBIS Assessment you may want to refer to the Dynamics: Gender page of your personalize report as it relates to this exercise. Either way, this workbook exercise will help you identify some of your deepest needs in a marriage relationship and communicate those needs to your partner. It will take about twenty to thirty minutes.

Listed below are some of the most common needs that people identify as being important in marriage. Rate how important each of these items is for you. If you wish to add other items not included in our list, please do so. As always, do this on your own before discussing it with your partner.

	Not that important						Very important
Admiration	1	2	3	4	5	6	7
Affection	1	2	3	4	5	6	7
Commitment	1	2	3	4	5	6	7
Companionship	1	2	3	4	5	6	7
Conversation	1	2	3	4	5	6	7
Financial support	1	2	3	4	5	6	7
Honesty	1	2	3	4	5	6	7
Intimacy	1	2	3	4	5	6	7
Personal space	1	2	3	4	5	6	7
Respect	1	2	3	4	5	6	7
Rootedness	1	2	3	4	5	6	7
Security	1	2	3	4	5	6	7
Sex	1	2	3	4	5	6	7
Shared activities	1	2	3	4	5	6	7
_____	1	2	3	4	5	6	7
_____	1	2	3	4	5	6	7

Now that you have completed rating the needs, rank them in order of importance. Next, share the results with your partner.

What needs do both of you identify as important?

Discuss what needs are most important to you personally. As you discuss them, explain what that need means to you. Men and women often mean different things even when they use the same word (e.g., intimacy).

Finally, discuss how each of your needs might change as you grow in marriage.

Exercise Twenty

IDENTIFYING YOUR HOT TOPICS

THIS EXERCISE WILL HELP YOU PUT your finger on those issues that are especially prone to cause conflict in your relationship. It will take about twenty minutes. And if you are using the SYMBIS Assessment, you'll see this spelled out in personalized terms on the Dynamics: Conflict page of your report.

Listed below are the common relationship issues that most couples will encounter from time to time over the course of the relationship. Rate how much of a problem each issue is for you right now. If you wish to add other areas not included in our list, please do so. As always, do this on your own before discussing it with your partner.

	Not at all a problem						Very much a problem
Careers	1	2	3	4	5	6	7
Children	1	2	3	4	5	6	7
Chores	1	2	3	4	5	6	7
Communication	1	2	3	4	5	6	7
Friends	1	2	3	4	5	6	7
Illness	1	2	3	4	5	6	7
In-laws	1	2	3	4	5	6	7
Jealousy	1	2	3	4	5	6	7
Money	1	2	3	4	5	6	7
Priorities	1	2	3	4	5	6	7
Recreation	1	2	3	4	5	6	7
Relatives	1	2	3	4	5	6	7
Religion	1	2	3	4	5	6	7
Sex	1	2	3	4	5	6	7
Sleep habits	1	2	3	4	5	6	7
_____	1	2	3	4	5	6	7
_____	1	2	3	4	5	6	7

Now that you have completed rating the issues, share the results with your partner. What issues are "hot" for both of you, and what issues are "hot" for one or the other of you? Next, discuss which issues might become more troublesome in the future and what you can do to calm the conflict before it erupts.

MONEY TALKS AND SO CAN WE

THIS EXERCISE WILL HELP YOU delve into money matters that will impact your marriage in countless ways. It may take a bit longer than some of the other exercises in this workbook, but it is immensely practical and will benefit you for decades.

YOUR FAMILY AND MONEY

You already know from earlier exercises that your family of origin shapes nearly everything you do. And how you relate to money is not an exception. So let's begin by having you simply note how money was treated, valued, and managed in your home growing up. How did your childhood shape your beliefs about money? Make a few notes here so that you can discuss it in a moment with your partner. Be sure to note how you think you are similar or different than your parents when it comes to money matters. And also note how you see money being managed in your home together.

_____

_____

_____

THE MONEY SELF-TEST

What follows is a series of statements for you to rate. There are no right or wrong answers, and don't try to answer how you think others might want you to. Be honest. This is a self-test that will help you and your partner get real about personal finances.

1. I feel comfortable talking about finances with my partner.

Never	Rarely	Sometimes	Often	Always

2. I pay bills on time.

Never	Rarely	Sometimes	Often	Always

3. I pay off my credit card balance every month.

Never	Rarely	Sometimes	Often	Always

4. I save a portion of my income every month.

Never	Rarely	Sometimes	Often	Always

5. I give a predetermined portion of my money to charities or my church every month.

Never	Rarely	Sometimes	Often	Always

6. I manage my money with a set budget that I follow.

Never	Rarely	Sometimes	Often	Always

7. I buy things on impulse.

Never	Rarely	Sometimes	Often	Always

8. Most people who know me well would say I'm a saver and rather tight with my money.

Never	Rarely	Sometimes	Often	Always

9. I know how much I have in my bank account at almost any given time.

Never	Rarely	Sometimes	Often	Always

10. I regularly keep track of what I spend and where I spend it.

Never	Rarely	Sometimes	Often	Always

11. When it comes to investing, I give serious thought to and study how I can invest my money for high returns in the long run.

Never	Rarely	Sometimes	Often	Always

Once you have completed this self-test, take a few minutes to talk with your partner about money matters. Begin by discussing how your families approached finances. And keep in mind that this discussion is simply about getting money matters on the table. It's not about judging each other's approaches. And as you compare your answers on your two self-tests, note each item where your answers are quite divergent.

Here are a few questions to help you organize your findings:

1. Do you have the same or different views on spending styles, credit, and debt?

_____

_____

2. Your views on giving and saving money and investing for the future?

_____

_____

3. Your views on working with a financial plan and budget?

_____

_____

DO YOU CLASH OVER CASH?

After this discussion, rank on the following continuum where the two of you might fall when it comes to money matters:

Out of sync   In sync

| 1 | 2 | 3 | 4 | 5 | 6 | 7 | 8 | 9 | 10 |

Don't be disturbed if you find you have many divergent views on finances as a couple. Most couples do. What matters is what you are going to do about it. What follows are practical suggestions to help you begin implementing a proven plan.

IF EITHER ONE OF YOU IS IN
DEBT, START DIGGING OUT

If you haven't done so already, each of you needs to be up front with the other about where you are personally on your finances as it relates to debt. We've seen many couples who get married only to discover that their partner has a significant amount of debt that was never disclosed beforehand. Don't allow this to happen to you, and don't hold back this kind of information from your partner. You will wrestle with trust issues for decades as a result of not being up front early on. And it's simple. It basically involves answering three primary questions:

1. Do you have credit card debt? If so, how much?
2. Do you have loans you are paying off? If so, how much?
3. Do you owe anyone money? If so, how much?

Now if either of you has financial debt, you need to devise a plan together for getting out of it as soon as possible. If the debt is significant, this may mean talking with a financial consultant who specializes in these matters. One of the most respected and successful do-it-yourself programs comes from Dave Ramsey, and you can visit his website at www.daveramsey.com. You'll want to implement a cash control system, for example, and you will find all the tools you need for this at his site. Digging out of debt is the first order of business in getting on your feet financially as a couple.

DESIGN A BUDGET

Whether you have debt or not, we strongly recommend that you design a budget together as a couple. Why? Because a budget allows you to control your money rather than the other way around. And it's not as bad as you might imagine. It begins by getting an accurate picture of your total income and then deciding how you will allocate it. Of course, this may be revised as circumstances change, but you've got to start somewhere. If you're working with a SYMBIS Facilitator, they can provide you with an Excel version of the budget worksheet that does all the math for you. If not, here's a budget worksheet that will help you get going:

Basic Budget Worksheet

CATEGORY	MONTHLY BUDGET AMOUNT	MONTHLY ACTUAL AMOUNT	DIFFERENCE BETWEEN ACTUAL AND BUDGET
INCOME:			
Salary/Wages			
Bonuses			
Investment Income			
Miscellaneous Income			
INCOME SUBTOTAL			
EXPENSES:			
Mortgage or Rent			
TV Cable			
Telephone			
Home Repairs/ Maintenance			
Car Payments			
Gasoline/Oil			
Auto Repairs/ Maintenance/Fees			
Other Transportation (tolls, bus, subway, etc.)			
Child Care			
Auto Insurance			

CATEGORY	MONTHLY BUDGET AMOUNT	MONTHLY ACTUAL AMOUNT	DIFFERENCE BETWEEN ACTUAL AND BUDGET
Home Owner's/ Renter's Insurance			
Computer Expense			
Entertainment/ Recreation			
Groceries			
Toiletries/Household Products			
Clothing			
Eating Out			
Tithe/Donations			
Health Care (medical/ dental/ vision, incl. insurance)			
Hobbies			
Interest Expense (mortgage, credit cards, fees)			
Magazines/ Newspapers			
Federal Income Tax			
State Income Tax			
Social Security/ Medicare Tax			
Personal Property Tax			
Pets			
Miscellaneous Expenses			
EXPENSES SUBTOTAL			

NET INCOME (INCOME LESS EXPENSES)			

Here's How to Use This Worksheet:

- Go through your checkbook or bills for the last two to three months and add and delete categories from the worksheet to fit your expenditures.

- Think about your hobbies and your habits and be sure to add categories for these expenses.

- Go through your pay stubs and calculate your average monthly gross pay. Do the same for any interest income, dividends, bonuses, or other miscellaneous income.

- For each expense category, try to determine a budget amount that realistically reflects your actual expenses while setting targeted spending levels that will enable you to save money.

- If an expense is incurred more or less often than monthly, convert it to a monthly amount when calculating the monthly budget amount. For instance, an auto expense that is billed every six months would be converted to monthly by dividing the six-month premium by six.

- Once you're comfortable with your expense categories and budgeted amounts, enter expenditures from your checkbook from the last month.

- Keep track of cash expenditures throughout the month and total and categorize these at the end of each month.

- Subtotal the income and expense categories. Subtract the total expenses from the total income to arrive at your net income.

- If the number is negative, your expenses are greater than your income. Your situation can probably be greatly improved by changing your spending habits.

- After you've tracked your actual spending for a month or two, analyze your spending to identify where you can comfortably make cuts.

- Once you've gotten the budgeting process in place, take an in-depth look at your largest spending categories, brainstorm about ways to reduce spending in specific categories, and set realistic goals.

Keep this in mind: One of the top reasons, if not *the* top reason, so many people fail at budgeting is attitude. If you think of it as a penny-pinching sacrifice instead of a means for achieving your financial goals and dreams, how long are you likely to stick with it? Many people refuse to budget because of budgeting's negative connotation. If you're one of these people, try thinking of it as a "spending plan" instead of a "budget." It's like the difference between going on a diet and eating healthily. One is negative and restrictive; the other is positive and allows you to indulge now and then and still achieve your goals.

TALK ABOUT YOUR FINANCIAL GOALS

Throughout your marriage you will talk about financial goals from time to time, but this is an important topic at the start as well. So take another moment or two to consider where you and your partner would like to be financially in another year, another five years, ten years, and so on. Here are some questions to generate this discussion:

1. What are your thoughts on owning your own home?
2. Have you considered how your finances will be impacted by having children?
3. Do you have a plan for paying off car loans?
4. What are your goals when it comes to giving money away and supporting causes you believe in?

If you are using the SYMBIS Assessment you will want to also refer to the Money Matrix personalized report. It provides an even deeper experience of some of the financial issues explored in this workbook exercise.

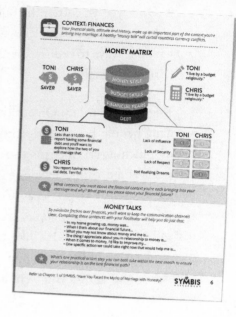

Exercise Twenty-Two

MIND READING

THIS EXERCISE WILL HELP YOU bring true and false assumptions you are making about your partner into the open so there are fewer surprises and conflicts. It will take about ten minutes.

Normally, trying to "mind read" what your partner is thinking is not a healthy habit (because it will lead you to jump to irrational conclusions). That's why in this exercise you will actually assess the accuracy of your assumptions before acting on them.

Here's how it works. The next time you sense that your partner is upset with you, pause for a moment and say, "I want to read your mind." Then tell him what you think he was saying to himself. For example, "I think you are mad about the way I left the bed this morning," or "I think you are upset because I wanted to watch TV instead of take a walk." Then say, "How accurate am I?" Your partner can then rate how accurate you are on a percentage scale. For example, he might say, "That's about 20 percent accurate," or "That's 100 percent accurate."

This simple exercise can be done anytime you sense that your partner is upset and you'd like to know if you are right about the reasons for it. Every couple mind reads every day. This exercise just makes that habit up front and more useful.

To get the feel of how this exercise works, consider how your partner was thinking or feeling about something in your relationship that happened within the last couple of days. Of course, this exercise is most helpful when used in the present tense (while you are in the midst of an experience), but to get the hang of it, you'll bring up something that's already happened—something that you never really processed but made assumptions about (e.g., you think he was upset when you didn't show up on time). Once you have that in mind, complete this sentence:

I think you were _____

_____

_____

Now, ask her how accurate you are in this assumption and note it on the following scale:

Completely Inaccurate   Right on the Money

| 1 | 2 | 3 | 4 | 5 | 6 | 7 | 8 | 9 | 10 |

Again, the point of this simple exercise is to diffuse your natural inclination to "mind read" by making your assumptions known. You'll be amazed how handy this can be in the midst of an intense conversation.

Exercise Twenty-Three

SHARING WITHHOLDS

THIS EXERCISE WILL HELP YOU and your partner keep a clean emotional slate and avoid needless conflicts. We call it "sharing withholds" because it gives you the chance to share thoughts and feelings you may have withheld from each other. It will take about ten to fifteen minutes, and many couples find it helpful to do this exercise on a weekly basis.

Begin by writing two things your partner has done in the last forty-eight hours that you sincerely appreciated but did not tell him. For example, "I appreciate the compliment you gave me as I got out of the car yesterday, and I never did tell you," or "I appreciate the help you gave me in writing my proposal last night, and I don't think you know how much that meant to me."

I appreciate . . .

_____

I appreciate . . .

_____

Next, write one thing your partner has done in the last forty-eight hours that irritated you, but which you did not say anything about. For example, "I didn't like it when you borrowed my umbrella without telling me," or "I didn't like it when you said nothing about the meal I prepared for us last night."

83

Once both of you have written your statements, take turns sharing them. One person shares all three statements one after the other—we recommend sandwiching the negative withhold between the two positives when you share them. Then the other person shares his or her three statements.

And here is an important part of this exercise: The person on the receiving end can say only "thank you" after each statement. That's all. Just "thank you." This rule allows couples to share something that bugs them without fearing a blowup or a defensive reaction. It also allows couples to receive critiques in the context of affirmation.

Here's another important piece to this exercise: Once you've both shared your withholds, neither of you can talk about the negative withhold you just heard for thirty minutes. Why? Because in a half hour's time you will have become more rational and thoughtful. At that point you can then ask your partner questions about it and are far less likely to have an emotional reaction. At that time, too, you may simply be inclined to offer an apology if appropriate. The point is not to stir up a fight where there was none. The point is to clear the "emotional land mines" from your marriage by keeping you current and not allowing painful wounds, even minor ones, to fester.

This exercise can be done weekly as we mentioned. Once you get the hang of it, you don't necessarily need to write your statements down, but it's often helpful. You may also want to agree on a routine time when you can do this exercise each week (e.g., Wednesdays after dinner) so one of you doesn't have to always initiate it. If you put this into practice by making it a weekly habit, we think you'll agree that sharing withholds can save you hundreds of hours of needless bickering.

Exercise Twenty-Four

CREATING A CLEAN SLATE

TO PARAPHRASE IVY BAKER PRIEST, the end may also be the beginning—if you start again with a clean slate. So if you are entering marriage for the second time, we want to help you do that through this workbook exercise.

Write a short history of your former relationship by completing the following sentence stems:

1. The things that initially attracted me to my first husband were . . .

_____

_____

2. I decided to marry my first husband because . . .

_____

_____

3. My first husband contributed to making our marriage work by . . .

_____

_____

4. I personally contributed to the relationship's difficulties by . . .

_____

_____

5. I still feel angry about . . .

_____

_____

6. I still feel guilty about . . .

_____

_____

7. I still feel sad about . . .

_____

_____

8. A lesson I've learned about marriage that I'll apply in my second marriage is . . .

_____

_____

9. What my first marriage taught me about myself is . . .

_____

_____

Once you have taken the time to seriously contemplate and respond to each of these items, set aside some meaningful time to discuss them with your partner. If he has been married before, you can take turns responding to each of these items.

Exercise Twenty-Five

REMARRIED WITH CHILDREN

SO YOU ARE ABOUT TO PLUNGE into a new marriage that comes prepackaged with children. Are you ready? Most people would say you're not fully equipped until you've devised a plan. In this exercise we offer a way to get you started in doing just that.

Below is a list of important pointers for building a successful combined family. Read through the list and rank the top half-dozen items you feel are most important for you. It is important to do this on your own at first without influence from your partner.

___ Start out in our own new place. This will eliminate turf squabbles, alleviate hurt feelings, and allow us to rid ourselves of the ghosts of the past.

___ Ease into the relationships with our children and let them develop gradually. Relationships do not develop on demand. Trust takes time.

___ Develop our own new traditions as a family. These will hasten our sense of belonging and connectedness as we develop familiar routines and special celebrations.

___ Negotiate differences instead of fighting over right and wrong. Whether we let the dog sleep at the foot of the bed or in the garage is not a matter of right or wrong but simply a difference in preference.

___ Maintain a special, planned, one-on-one time that allows our relationship to grow and be nourished in the midst of learning to parent together.

___ Support our children's access to both biological parents. We do not want our children to be caught in the middle, nor do we want them to be emotionally torn apart.

___ Adults in both households will make direct contact with each other to work out residential schedules with input from the children. We will not talk to each other through the children.

___ We understand that much of a child's anger comes from changes and losses they have not chosen. Sharing a parent, a room, or toy with stepsiblings; going to a new school; missing your other parent, friends, and former neighborhood; having unfamiliar food; adjusting to new rules — all make for some guaranteed difficulties that we will work to understand.

___ We will do all we can to learn about the dynamics of stepfamily situations. We will read books, talk to other stepparents, and attend seminars that will sharpen our skills as we work together as a parental team.

___ Biological parents and ex-spouses will strive to be cooperative coparents with one another. We will compartmentalize our anger and hurt so we can cooperate on issues regarding the children's wellbeing. We know that if our conflict continues, the children will suffer.

Once you have ranked your items, compare notes with your partner. Discuss the items each of you checked and explain why. Then use these items to devise a plan for building your combined family together.

Exercise Twenty-Six

YOUR SPIRITUAL JOURNEY

THIS EXERCISE WILL HELP YOU and your partner share your individual pilgrimages. It will take about fifteen to twenty-five minutes.

Part of cultivating spiritual intimacy comes from merging two individual journeys. We are all beginners when it comes to spiritual development, but each of us has come from a different place and traveled a different road to meet where we are today. You may have grown up in a religious home learning Bible verses, going to Sunday school, and studying at a Christian college. Or maybe you never went to church while growing up and are just becoming grounded in your faith. Whatever your story, take a moment to gather your thoughts about your own spiritual quest. Then make a few notes of some of the significant mile markers.

_____

_____

_____

_____

_____

_____

_____

_____

Next, take a moment to complete this brief quiz.

Agree	Disagree	Spouses should ...
☐	☐	Pray together every day.
☐	☐	Study the Bible together regularly.
☐	☐	Discuss spiritual issues.
☐	☐	Go to the same church.
☐	☐	Agree on theology.
☐	☐	Pay a tithe.
☐	☐	Pray for each other.
☐	☐	Leave each other's spiritual life up to God.
☐	☐	Have the same level of spiritual maturity.
☐	☐	Attend church at least once a week.

Once you have gathered your thoughts and completed the quiz, share your journey with your partner. Discuss what has brought you to where you are today. Also, compare how each of you responded to the quiz. Use it as a springboard to a deeper discussion of how each of you views spiritual matters.

Next, seek to understand how both you and your partner love God. This can be revolutionary for some couples. In his helpful book *Sacred Pathways* (Zondervan, 2002), Gary Thomas describes nine ways we tend to relate to God. Rank the top two or three styles that fit you best. Then try to predict your partner's top pathways before comparing notes.

Me	My Partner	
☐	☐	*The Traditionalist* loves God through rituals, sacraments, and symbols throughout the year.
☐	☐	*The Visionary* loves God by dreaming a great dream to accomplish great things.
☐	☐	*The Socialite* loves God best around other people, confiding in them and being accountable to them.
☐	☐	*The Intellectual* seeks God with his or her mind by considering a new theological concept.
☐	☐	*The Caregiver* loves God by being compassionate and loving others even if it means significant sacrifice.
☐	☐	*The Contemplative* seeks to love God in a quiet pursuit of journaling and reflection.
☐	☐	*The Activist* is at war with injustice and loves God by fighting it.
☐	☐	*The Naturalist* feels closest to God in the out-of-doors in the midst of creation.
☐	☐	*The Worshiper* is inspired by joyful celebration and music.

Now, jot down some specific ways these pathways are manifested in your life. If you are a Contemplative, for example, what do you like to do, where do you like to go, and how much time do you like to spend, to be close to God?

_____

_____

_____

Once you and your partner have both noted the top two or three styles that fit you best, spend a few minutes comparing them and discuss what you might learn from each other's pathways.

If you are using the SYMBIS Assessment you will want to also refer to the Dynamics: Spirituality portion of your personalized report. It provides further exploration of how your personalities and desires impact your spiritual journey together.

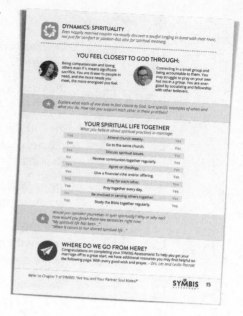

IMPROVING YOUR SERVE

THIS EXERCISE WILL HELP YOU and your partner cultivate a soulful marriage by reaching out to others. It will take about ten to fifteen minutes.

Here are a few of the ways couples have practiced the fine art of serving others:

- Volunteering in a youth group
- Supporting someone's education
- Taking care of a shut-in's lawn
- Welcoming new people to the neighborhood
- Doing short-term relief trips overseas
- Sending helpful books to people

Take a moment to list a few ways that you and your partner might reach out together as a team. Work on your own and be as creative as you can before sharing your thoughts with your partner.

Now compare your list with your partner's. Combine your lists and begin to rank the items in order of what both of you might like to do as a team. Once you have a couple of things that seem like they might fit your joint style, discuss in more detail what they might actually look like.

1. How would the two of you actually live out these forms of service?

_____

_____

_____

2. What do you think reaching out to others might do for your marriage?

_____

_____

_____

Exercise Twenty-Eight

STUDY YOUR SPOUSE

THIS EXERCISE WILL HELP YOU understand your partner's unique needs now and in the future. It will take about five to ten minutes *each day*.

No one can play as significant a role in encouraging your partner as you. No one can meet her needs better than you. But to be effective, you must study your partner by paying careful attention to his needs, desires, and aspirations.

This exercise is simply a prayer. It need not involve any sharing or discussion with your partner. It simply asks you to study and pray.

> *God, our Creator, you were there when my partner was formed. You knit him together in his mother's womb. You know his every thought, need, and desire. You are acquainted with all his ways. Enlighten me. Teach me to know this complicated man you have given me to love.*

Record any of your thoughts or observations below as you consider how you can better understand and study your soul mate. How does your new understanding of your partner change the way you treat him? Here are a few follow-up questions to help you structure your thoughts and review the content of *Saving Your Second Marriage Before It Starts*:

1. What can you keep in mind about his expectations (shaped by the family he came from) that will allow you to have a deeper understanding of him?

_____

_____

_____

_____

2. As you think about his definition of love (what makes him feel loved by you) as well as the three essential ingredients of love (passion, intimacy, and commitment), what are the actions you can intentionally take and observations you can make to express your love to him?

_____

_____

_____

_____

3. When you think about "the habit of happiness" as it relates to him, what can you keep in mind about his internal "self-talk" and what helps him to keep a positive attitude?

_____

_____

_____

_____

4. What kinds of conversations does he most enjoy, and when are you most likely to experience them?

_____

_____

_____

_____

_____

5. As you bridge the gender gap in your marriage, what will serve you well to keep in mind about him as a man?

_____

_____

_____

_____

_____

6. What issues are most likely to result in frustration and tension for him (what are his hot topics?), and what can you learn to do better to resolve conflicts with him?

_____

_____

_____

_____

_____

7. As you consider his spiritual journey, what can you do to help him carve out a path to God that is meaningful in your marriage?

_____

_____

_____

_____

_____

Study your partner. Listen to him, talk to him. And every day, pray this simple prayer, asking God to help you understand him better.

SESSIONS

For Group or Couple Discussion with the Group Video Series

INTRODUCTION

STUDYING THIS MATERIAL IN A GROUP with other couples is one of the best ways to make it stick—and have a lot of fun in the process. To that end, we've created this nine-session group discussion guide. Most people feel this is just about the right length for a group series. Though we've created this discussion guide for group or classroom use, it is also adaptable for individual couple's study if you and your partner prefer to go through the questions on your own or are unable to connect with others who are studying the same curriculum.

Before your group meetings, it would be helpful for you to read the assigned chapters associated with the session, but this is not required. Obviously, you are going to get more out of the discussion if you've "done your homework." So if you can make the time to read the chapters, great! If not, don't worry. You can still join in on the discussion (it doesn't rely on having read the chapters), and you don't need to feel an ounce of guilt. The purpose is to enjoy the interaction and to learn from it. You can always read the chapters later, if you wish.

Here's a quick glimpse at what you'll be doing in each group session. We've designed each session to last about an hour, but you can take more or less time as your schedule dictates.

JUST FOR FUN
(4 MINUTES)

Each session begins with a question or activity that is "just for fun"—a kind of icebreaker. These are just to get the wheels turning and to help you connect as you come together as a group.

VIDEO NOTES
(15 - 30 MINUTES)

In addition to hearing from Les and Leslie Parrott, each session will include two brief video segments featuring several real-life couples who are exploring these issues just as you are. As you watch the DVD or digital session, feel free to fill in the content points supplied, in addition to jotting down your notes, questions, and reactions in the space provided.

EXPLORING YOUR WORKBOOK EXERCISE
(15 - 20 MINUTES)

Each of the sessions will rely on an exercise from this workbook. You will typically spend time within the group session doing the exercise, then discussing it. While of course it would be helpful to have the exercises completed beforehand, you may do them within your group if you wish. We've selected exercises that will not put anyone on the spot or force anyone to share information they don't want to. Of course, your group may elect to use other exercises from this workbook to discuss if you wish. That's up to you and your group. But we will point you to the exercises in this workbook that we feel are most suitable.

TIME TO DISCUSS
(20 MINUTES)

The list of questions you'll find in this section is designed to spark ideas, reactions, and real-life examples. As you interact, remember that a key ingredient to successful group discussion is vulnerability. This doesn't mean you have to say anything you don't want to. It's just that, typically, the more transparent you are, the more meaningful the experience will be, and the more open others will be as well. Vulnerability begets vulnerability. However, we caution you not to use this time to gripe about your partner in some way. Don't embarrass each other by dragging out dirty laundry you know would upset your partner. You want to be genuine and vulnerable, but not at the expense of your partner's feelings.

Another key ingredient in these discussions is specificity. You'll gain much more out of this time when you use specific examples with each other. So with this in mind, we will remind you to "be specific" every so often.

Finally, if you are a group facilitator, don't feel that you need to follow the order given or even use every question. Let the dynamics of the discussion be your guide.

YOUR SYMBIS ASSESSMENT

If you are using the SYMBIS Assessment, this section will direct you to the pertinent pages of your report and help you explore the personal information on these pages within the context of each video session. While we have placed this section toward the end of the session flow, feel free to move it earlier in your session if you like. (Note: No time allotment has been suggested for this component. If you include an assessment discussion as part of your session and are restricted to an hour of group time, adjust the other time frames accordingly.)

TAKING TIME AS A COUPLE

Finally, we've included suggestions for ways you can take this group experience into your week together as a couple. We encourage you to further discuss and apply the material as a way to connect and grow together. And of course you can also read the book together or individually if you can make the time. Again, no pressure or guilt.

One more thing: Relax. Have fun. And enjoy the opportunity to master life skills that will improve your relationship and help you develop a strong foundation for a marriage that will last a lifetime.

Session One

ARE YOU READY TO GET MARRIED AGAIN?

WHETHER IT'S ONE PARTNER or both who are entering a second marriage, being fully prepared for the unique challenges remarriage presents is essential. This session will help you explore critical marriage issues that you'll want to address—so you are both ready for a relationship that lasts a lifetime.

JUST FOR FUN
(4 MINUTES)

Describe your first impression of each other. What was that first encounter like, and how has your first impression changed from then to now? How has it remained the same?

VIDEO SEGMENT #1 NOTES
(7 MINUTES)

- Reasons to _____ remarry

- The most important reason to get married again is
  _____.

EXPLORING YOUR WORKBOOK EXERCISE
(15 MINUTES)

Within your group, complete exercise 2 in your workbook (page 18). Discuss your responses with the group. Remember, there's no need to disclose anything you feel is too personal or private, but share what you learned about yourself and your relationship as a result of completing this exercise.

VIDEO SEGMENT #2 NOTES
(7 MINUTES)

- _____ readiness

- _____ readiness

- Your marriage can only be as _____ as the two of you.

TIME TO DISCUSS
(20 MINUTES)

1. What have you heard about remarriage (from friends, family, media, and so on)?

_____

_____

_____

_____

_____

Group
Video
Series

2. In the video session you just watched, what comments from couples in this session do you most resonate with and why?

_____

_____

_____

_____

_____

3. What does "relational readiness for remarriage" mean to you? How do you know when the relationship is in a good place to move into remarriage?

_____

_____

_____

_____

_____

4. In your opinion, what is likely to be a unique challenge you might face as a couple involved in a remarriage?

_____

_____

_____

_____

_____

YOUR SYMBIS ASSESSMENT

If you are using the SYMBIS Assessment, review the Context: Remarriage section (page 7A) of your report. Explore your individual motivations to remarry; how are they similar and different? Of course, you will only have information on this page if you are marrying again. If it's a first marriage for one of you, this will still be a helpful conversation. Do the same thing for the portion about your remarriage readiness.

TAKING TIME AS A COUPLE

To further explore whether you are ready for remarriage, spend some time this week as a couple reading chapter 1 and completing exercise 1 in the workbook. If you have time, also discuss the reflection questions with your partner.

Session Two

HAVE YOU FACED THE MYTHS OF MARRIAGE WITH HONESTY?

What you believe about marriage will become the fuel for your behavior in marriage. For this reason, exploring the myths of marriage is essential.

JUST FOR FUN
(4 MINUTES)

Whether you are doing this as an individual couple or as a small group of couples, take a moment to name one of the most romantic movies you've ever seen. It could be *The Notebook*, *The Fault in Our Stars*, *Sleepless in Seattle*, *Casablanca*, *Titanic*, *Father of the Bride*, *When Harry Met Sally*, or any of the hundreds of other romantic stories. What makes this movie so romantic to you? Do you see yourself in it? From your perspective, what's the primary message of the movie? If you don't like this line of questioning, name a romantic movie that you didn't like. Why?

VIDEO SEGMENT #1 NOTES
(17 MINUTES)

- Your beliefs are the fuel for your behavior.

- Myth #1: We expect the _____ from marriage.

- _____ Rules

- _____ Roles

EXPLORING YOUR WORKBOOK EXERCISE
(20 MINUTES)

Within your small group, take time to complete exercise 4 in your workbook (page 24). This exercise explores making conscious your understanding of the roles both you and your partner have in a marriage. If you are comfortable, share with the group: What insights did you have while doing this exercise? How have your families of origin influenced your understanding of roles? What items did you have to renegotiate?

VIDEO SEGMENT #2 NOTES
(12 MINUTES)

- Myth #2: Everything _____ will get better.

- Myth #3: Everything _____ will disappear.

- Myth #4: Adjustment to married life occurs more _____ in remarriage.

- Myth #5: My spouse will make me _____.

- If you try to build intimacy with another person before getting whole on your own, all your relationships become an attempt to complete yourself.

- A-Frame Relationship = overly _____

- H-Frame Relationship = overly _____

- M-Frame Relationship = _____

TIME TO DISCUSS
(20 MINUTES)

1. Which ideas expressed in the video were new to you?

_____

_____

_____

_____

2. Which concept talked about in today's session can you apply to your relationship?

_____

_____

_____

_____

3. In what areas of your life is your relationship operating as an **A**, **H**, or **M**?

_____

_____

_____

_____

4. What other myths do couples bring to the marriage relationship?

_____

_____

_____

_____

YOUR SYMBIS ASSESSMENT

If you are using the SYMBIS Assessment, review the Context section of your report (pages 5–7). What myths of marriage might you debunk as a result of seeing this personal information on these pages? For example, "we are going to do everything together," is a common misbelief. Page 7 of your report will make this plain.

TAKING TIME AS A COUPLE

To further explore marital myths you may have believed, spend some time this week as a couple reading chapter 2 and completing exercises 1, 3, 5, 6, and 7 in the workbook. If you have time, also discuss the reflection questions with your partner.

Session Three

CAN YOU IDENTIFY YOUR LOVE STYLE?

Do you have a crystal clear concept of love? And do you see it the same way as your partner? This session will ensure that you get on the same page as you write your love story together.

JUST FOR FUN
(4 MINUTES)

Whether you are doing this as an individual couple or as a small group of couples, take a moment to answer these questions together: If you were designing a recipe for the perfect romantic day, and money wasn't an object, what would go into it and why? What would you do together to cultivate romance for twenty-four hours with an unlimited budget? As you reflect on this daydream, consider how romance relates to love. In other words, what percentage of married love do you think involves romance?

VIDEO SEGMENT #1 NOTES
(13 MINUTES)

- Passion is the _____ component of love.

- Intimacy is the _____ component of love.

- Commitment is the _____ component of love.

EXPLORING YOUR WORKBOOK EXERCISE
(15 MINUTES)

Within your small group, take time to complete exercise 8 in your workbook (page 35). This exercise should help you define love in your own terms and compare your definition with your partner's. What qualities of love were most important to you? To your partner? Discuss with the group how your definition of love compared to your partner's.

VIDEO SEGMENT #2 NOTES
(17 MINUTES)

• How to cultivate passion (for women): _____

• How to cultivate intimacy (for men): _____

• How to cultivate commitment (for both men and women):

_____

TIME TO DISCUSS
(20 MINUTES)

1. Which idea presented in today's session did you find most interesting? Why?

_____

_____

_____

_____

2. In your love life right now, which component of love seems most powerful: passion, intimacy, or commitment? Why?

_____

_____

_____

_____

3. In what ways can you nurture each component of love: passion, intimacy, and commitment?

_____

_____

_____

_____

4. Why is it important to remember that love is constantly changing and growing?

_____

_____

_____

_____

YOUR SYMBIS ASSESSMENT

If you are using the SYMBIS Assessment, review the Dynamics: Love section (page 10) of your report. How do your unique personalities view love in practical terms? Explore your two unique definitions of love and the top three ingredients that matter most to each of you.

TAKING TIME AS A COUPLE

In order to better understand your love style, spend some time this week as a couple reading chapter 3 and completing exercises 10 and 11 in the workbook. If you have time, also discuss the reflection questions with your partner.

Session Four

HAVE YOU DEVELOPED THE HABIT OF HAPPINESS?

This habit can make or break a marriage. And it's important to remember that it has little to do with your partner and everything to do with you. In other words, an upbeat attitude is highly contagious.

JUST FOR FUN
(4 MINUTES)

Whether you are doing this as an individual couple or as a small group of couples, take a moment to answer these questions together: Consider a time when you had "one of those days"—a time when nothing seemed to go as planned. Looking back on it, can you find any humor in it? If your experience was written into a sitcom, what would the name of the show be called and why? Now, think about how you typically respond when unexpected circumstances interrupt your plans. Anything you'd like to change about your attitude in these times?

VIDEO SEGMENT #1 NOTES
(10 MINUTES)

- The one habit that can make or break your relationship is the capacity to adjust to things _____ your control.

- The most important quality of a marriageable person is the habit of _____.

EXPLORING YOUR WORKBOOK EXERCISE
(15 MINUTES)

Within your group, complete exercise 12 in your workbook (page 49). Share with others how you see your attitude shaping the moods of your marriage. What types of things affect your mood? What negative self-talk have you used, and how can you help your partner avoid negative self-talk that she might use?

VIDEO SEGMENT #2 NOTES
(9 MINUTES)

- The three toxins that can seep into a marriage relationship:

  _____ , _____ ,

  _____

TIME TO DISCUSS
(20 MINUTES)

1. What struck you most about today's session?

_____

_____

_____

_____

_____

2. When are you most likely to blame your partner?

_____

_____

_____

_____

_____

3. Do you think the most important quality of a marriageable person is the habit of happiness? Why or why not?

_____

_____

_____

_____

_____

4. What keeps you from *choosing* to be happy?

_____

_____

_____

_____

_____

YOUR SYMBIS ASSESSMENT

If you are using the SYMBIS Assessment, review the Dynamics: Attitude section (page 11) of your report. How would each of you describe your abilities to adjust to things beyond your control? In other words, how adaptable and resilient do you see yourselves being when faced with a challenge?

TAKING TIME AS A COUPLE

To further explore how your attitudes can affect your marriage, spend some time this week as a couple reading chapter 4 and completing exercises 13 and 14 in the workbook. If you have time, also discuss the reflection questions with your partner.

Session Five

CAN YOU SAY WHAT YOU MEAN AND UNDERSTAND WHAT YOU HEAR?

---

*Communication is the lifeline of every marriage.
But too often the lines of communication between
couples get crossed. Rest assured that this session will
help you speak each other's language fluently.*

JUST FOR FUN
(4 MINUTES)

If you are doing this as a small group of couples, take a moment to play the "whisper" game. One of you begins by whispering something (at least three sentences long)—it can be about anything (what you had for lunch, what you like to do on vacation, your idea of a dream wedding)—and the task is to convey the message around the entire group. You can't ask a person to repeat the message. You simply have to whisper to the next person what you heard. You'll be surprised by how the message ends up. If you are doing this session as an individual couple, talk about a time when you encountered a major miscommunication. What happened?

VIDEO SEGMENT #1 NOTES
(12 MINUTES)

- Men _____ talk.

- Women _____ talk.

- Communication Basics

- Skill #1: _____ content.

EXPLORING YOUR WORKBOOK EXERCISE
(15 MINUTES)

Within your small group, complete exercise 15 in your workbook (page 57). Compare your score with your partner's and discuss how well each of you is communicating. If you are comfortable, share with your group areas in which you can improve your communication.

VIDEO SEGMENT #2 NOTES
(7 MINUTES)

- Communication Basics

- Skill #2: _____ feeling.

- Without being genuine, the best communication techniques in the world will fall flat.

TIME TO DISCUSS
(20 MINUTES)

1. Which ideas presented in today's session were new to you?

_____

_____

_____

_____

_____

2. Which concept presented in this session seems most difficult for you to put into practice?

_____

_____

_____

_____

_____

3. Empathy involves using your head *and* your heart. Which do you tend to use more — your head or your heart? How can you begin to cultivate using both in your interactions with your partner?

_____

_____

_____

_____

_____

4. When do you feel most understood? When do you feel least understood? In what ways can you better communicate your own feelings about being understood?

_____

_____

_____

_____

_____

YOUR SYMBIS ASSESSMENT

If you are using the SYMBIS Assessment, review the Dynamics: Communication section (page 12) of your report. How would each of you describe your personal "talk styles" (which descriptors do you resonate with most)? From the list on this page, what are the two most important things that your partner needs to know about communicating with you? What is one practical thing you each will do to improve your communication skills?

TAKING TIME AS A COUPLE

To learn more about successful communication in your marriage, spend some time this week as a couple reading chapter 5 and completing exercises 16 and 17 in the workbook. If you have time, also discuss the reflection questions with your partner.

Session Six

HAVE YOU BRIDGED THE GENDER GAP?

Everybody knows that men and women are different. But what most newlywed couples don't realize, until they cross the proverbial threshold, is just how pronounced that difference is. This session will help make that transition much easier.

JUST FOR FUN
(10 MINUTES)

If you are studying this curriculum with other couples, divide into two groups: men in one group and women in another. In each group, appoint a facilitator and a secretary. Answer the question, "What do you want the other gender to know about your gender?" What insights do you gain from hearing what the other group has to say? If you and your partner are completing this on your own, discuss the same question with each other.

VIDEO SEGMENT #1 NOTES
(11 MINUTES)

- How men and women solve problems:

- Men want to _____ it.

- Women want to _____ it.

EXPLORING YOUR WORKBOOK EXERCISE
(20 MINUTES)

Within your group, complete exercise 19 in your workbook (page 67). This exercise should help you communicate your deepest needs to your partner. Share with the group the needs that were most important to you. How did these needs compare with those of your partner? How do you see your needs changing as you grow in your marriage?

VIDEO SEGMENT #2 NOTES
(10 MINUTES)

• Men need _____ activity.

• Women need to be _____.

TIME TO DISCUSS
(15 MINUTES)

1. What ideas did you hear today that were new to you?

_____

_____

_____

_____

_____

2. What general gender differences have you experienced in your relationship?

_____

_____

_____

_____

_____

3. How can these gender differences cause conflict in your marriage?

_____

_____

_____

_____

_____

4. What steps can you take to celebrate the differences you both bring to your marriage?

_____

_____

_____

_____

_____

YOUR SYMBIS ASSESSMENT

If you are using the SYMBIS Assessment, review the Dynamics: Gender section (page 13) of your report. How do you feel about the statements describing what your partner needs from you? What's one practical way that each of you can meet this particular need— especially once you are married? Also, note your top two needs and discuss why they are important to each of you.

TAKING TIME AS A COUPLE

To further explore how gender differences affect your marriage, spend some time this week as a couple reading chapter 6 and completing exercise 18 in the workbook. If you have time, also discuss the reflection questions with your partner.

Session Seven

DO YOU KNOW HOW TO FIGHT A GOOD FIGHT?

Conflict is inevitable. No matter how "in love" a couple is, friction eventually emerges. But the savvy couple knows how to use this conflict to their advantage. This session will show you how.

JUST FOR FUN
(4 MINUTES)

Sometimes people fight about the silliest things—like an insignificant detail in a story they are telling, how someone is driving the car, etc. What's the craziest conflict you have ever heard of and why? Also, have you ever encountered a conflict because you were convinced you were right about something and it turned out you weren't? If so, are you willing to share it?

VIDEO SEGMENT #1 NOTES
(18 MINUTES)

- Negative feelings that get buried have a high rate of resurrection.

EXPLORING YOUR WORKBOOK EXERCISE
(15 MINUTES)

Within your group, complete exercise 23 in your workbook (page 83). The skills learned from this exercise should help you and your partner avoid needless conflicts by remaining emotionally open with one another. If you are comfortable, share with the group how you felt when sharing withholds with your partner.

VIDEO SEGMENT #2 NOTES
(14 MINUTES)

- What to avoid in conflict: _____,

  _____, _____,

  _____

- XYZ Formula: In situation X, when you do Y, I feel Z.

- A great way to turn a _____

  into a _____

TIME TO DISCUSS
(20 MINUTES)

1. What causes the biggest conflicts in your relationship?

_____

_____

_____

_____

_____

2. How do you usually handle conflict?

_____

_____

_____

_____

_____

3. As you were growing up, how did your family typically handle conflict? What habits have you taken with you into your adult life?

_____

_____

_____

_____

_____

4. What "conflict habits" have you brought to your new relationship?

_____

_____

_____

_____

_____

YOUR SYMBIS ASSESSMENT

If you are using the SYMBIS Assessment, review the Dynamics: Conflict section (page 14) of your report. What statements within each of your individual "fight types" do you resonate with most? Which of your "personal conflict challenges" do you believe will be the most difficult and why? As you review your "hot topics" together, explore practical ways to alleviate the tension from the top two or three.

TAKING TIME AS A COUPLE

To further explore how to handle conflict in your marriage, spend some time this week as a couple reading chapter 7 and completing exercises 21 and 22 in the workbook. If you have time, also discuss the reflection questions with your partner.

Session Eight

DO YOU KNOW HOW TO BLEND A FAMILY?

IF YOU ARE MARRYING for the second time, you already know there are special challenges that are unique to your situation—especially if you are blending a family. This session is specifically for you.

JUST FOR FUN
(4 MINUTES)

Perhaps the modern-day iconic image of a second marriage situation is found in the 1970s sitcom *The Brady Bunch*. If you've seen the show, most likely in reruns, take a moment to talk about it. What are some of the memories you have from watching this program? And what, if anything, did the show have to say about a second marriage where kids are involved? If you haven't seen the show, talk about how the media generally portrays blended families.

VIDEO SEGMENT #1 NOTES
(9 MINUTES)

- Takes a minimum of _____ years

- Completing your own _____ business

- Being _____ to your ex

- Be the _____ disciplinarian.

- _____ for the nonbiological spouse

- You can't _____ the missing parent.

- Take a _____ course.

- Give _____ to the children and biological parent.

EXPLORING YOUR WORKBOOK EXERCISE
(20 MINUTES)

Within your group, take time to complete exercise 25 in your workbook (page 87). This exercise will help you determine what is most important for you in building a successful combined family. Discuss your responses with your partner before sharing with the group. Remember, there's no need to disclose anything you feel is too personal or private.

VIDEO SEGMENT #2 NOTES
(6 MINUTES)

- Make the new _____ paramount.

- Begin _____ family traditions.

- Respect _____ family traditions.

- Hold a _____ meeting.

- Protect everyone's _____ space.

- Don't _____ into having your own child together.

TIME TO DISCUSS
(20 MINUTES)

1. If you are the biological parent, what is one specific thing you can do to improve the blending process? Is there anything about your personal situation that will make blending your family more difficult?

_____

_____

_____

_____

2. Discipline is a big issue in blended families. If you are the biological parent, how can you take some concrete steps to be the primary disciplinarian?

_____

_____

_____

_____

3. If you are a stepparent, it can sometimes be tough to give your spouse time alone with his or her biological children. What can you do to feel good about this and ensure that it happens?

_____

_____

_____

_____

_____

4. Consider building new family traditions and activities into your blended family. What might they be? How can you respect the old traditions while building new ones?

_____

_____

_____

_____

YOUR SYMBIS ASSESSMENT

If you are using the SYMBIS Assessment, review the Context: Blending a Family section (page 7A) of your report. If one or both of you are bringing a child into the relationship, explore the information related to how the two of you will blend a family. Which of the statements is most important to you and why.

TAKING TIME AS A COUPLE

To further explore the topic of blending a family, take time this week as a couple reading chapter 8 and completing exercise 24 in the workbook.

Session Nine

ARE YOU AND YOUR PARTNER SOUL MATES?

You can do everything right in marriage and still wake up one morning and wonder, "Is this it?" You will continually be looking for depth and meaning in your relationship until you explore your spiritual nature — how the two of you walk together with God. This session will show you how to do just that.

JUST FOR FUN
(4 MINUTES)

Research shows that married couples who pray together enjoy a better sex life. What do you think of that? Why do you think this is so? And what does it say to you about the spiritual aspect of a married couple's life together?

VIDEO SEGMENT #1 NOTES
(7 MINUTES)

- On a scale of 1 to 10, most churchgoing couples rate the importance of spiritual intimacy as a 9 or 10, yet rate the level of satisfaction with their spiritual intimacy as a 2 or 3.
- Couples who pray together report higher satisfaction with their sex lives.

EXPLORING YOUR WORKBOOK EXERCISE
(15 MINUTES)

Within your group, complete exercise 27 in your workbook (page 93). This exercise explores reaching out to others as a way to strengthen your marriage. What are some activities you and your partner came up with to serve others? How do you think this service will impact your marriage?

VIDEO SEGMENT #2 NOTES
(8 MINUTES)

• When it comes to cultivating spiritual intimacy together, every couple has their own unique style.

TIME TO DISCUSS
(20 MINUTES)

1. On a scale of 1 to 10, how important is spiritual intimacy in your marriage? Explain your answer.

_____

_____

_____

_____

_____

2. On that same scale of 1 to 10, how satisfied are you with your current level of spiritual intimacy? Explain your answer.

_____

_____

_____

_____

_____

3. What are you presently doing in the area of shared service?

_____

_____

_____

_____

4. What is one thing you can do as a couple to strengthen the spiritual aspect of your relationship?

_____

_____

_____

_____

_____

YOUR SYMBIS ASSESSMENT

If you are using the SYMBIS Assessment, review the Dynamics: Spirituality section (page 15) of your report. How would you elaborate on the descriptions at the top of this page? What do you do in practical terms to draw closer to God? Would you expect your partner to do the same? Why or why not? Review "your spiritual life together." What practices do you agree with most? What practices do you two need to discuss in greater depth and why?

TAKING TIME AS A COUPLE

To further explore the spiritual nature of your marriage, spend some time this week as a couple reading chapter 9 and completing exercises 26 and 28 in the workbook. If you have time, also discuss the reflection questions with your partner.

GIVE THE VERY BEST TO

You won't find a more personalized and powerful pre-marriage assessment than SYMBIS.

"The SYMBIS Assessment rocks! We learned so much about our relationship and feel incredibly confident about our future together."
-Toni & Chris

Get your personalized 15-page report!

YOUR RELATIONSHIP

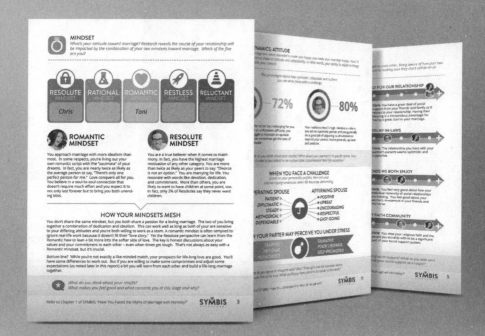

EVERYTHING YOU NEED TO KNOW ABOUT:

- **Your Personalities** – *discover your strengths*
- **Your Love Life** – *cultivate deeper passion*
- **Your Fight Types** – *discover your "hot topics"*
- **Your Talk Styles** – *crack your intimacy codes*
- **Your Money Methods** – *kick financial woes to the curb*

And so much more. **Plus***, it works seamlessly with
the SYMBIS book and his/her workbooks.*

Take the assessment: **SYMBISassessment.com**

YOUR ONE-STOP SHOP FOR
PRE-MARRIAGE

We've got everything you
need to launch lifelong love.

LesandLeslie.com

book

MARRIAGE
MENTORING
.COM

training

SYMBIS

SAVING YOUR MARRIAGE BEFORE IT STARTS

A S S E S S M E N T

Report for:

TONI DAY & CHRIS CRARY
Date Completed: 9/12/2014

Prepared by:
DRS. LES AND LESLIE PARROTT
info@LesandLeslie.com
206.123.4321

SYMBISAssessment.com

assessment

*remarriage
book*

DVD

his & hers
workbooks

SEVEN SESSIONS

SAVING YOUR
MARRIAGE
BEFORE IT STARTS

Seven Questions to Ask
Before — and After — You Marry

Drs. Les & Leslie Parrott

ZONDERVAN
DVD

WORKBOOK FOR MEN
Includes 24 Self-Tests and Group Discussion Guide

SAVING YOUR
MARRIAGE
BEFORE IT STARTS

Seven Questions to Ask Before — and After — You Marry

Drs. Les & Leslie Parrott
#1 New York Times Bestselling Authors

NEWLY EXPANDED EDITION

WORKBOOK FOR WOMEN
Includes 24 Self-Tests and Group Discussion Guide

SAVING YOUR
MARRIAGE
BEFORE IT STARTS

Seven Questions to Ask Before — and After — You Remarry

SYMBIS

Drs. Les & Leslie Parrott
#1 New York Times Bestselling Authors

NEWLY EXPANDED EDITION

Bible
studies

WORKBOOK FOR MEN
Includes 24 Self-Tests and Group Discussion Guide

SAVING YOUR
SECOND
MARRIAGE
BEFORE IT STARTS

Nine Questions to Ask Before — and After — You Remarry

SYMBIS

Drs. Les & Leslie Parrott
#1 New York Times Bestselling Authors

NEWLY EXPANDED EDITION

WORKBOOK FOR WOMEN
Includes 24 Self-Tests and Group Discussion Guide

SAVING YOUR
SECOND
MARRIAGE
BEFORE IT STARTS

Nine Questions to Ask Before — and After — You Remarry

SYMBIS

Drs. Les & Leslie Parrott
#1 New York Times Bestselling Authors

NEWLY EXPANDED EDITION

SAVING YOUR
SECOND
MARRIAGE
BEFORE IT STARTS

Nine Questions to Ask
Before — and After — You Marry

NINE SESSIONS

Drs. Les & Leslie Parrott

ZONDERVAN
DVD

remarriage
DVD

remarriage
workbooks